Saving Culture from Disaster

Elise Wallace

✳ Smithsonian

S0-BFB-027

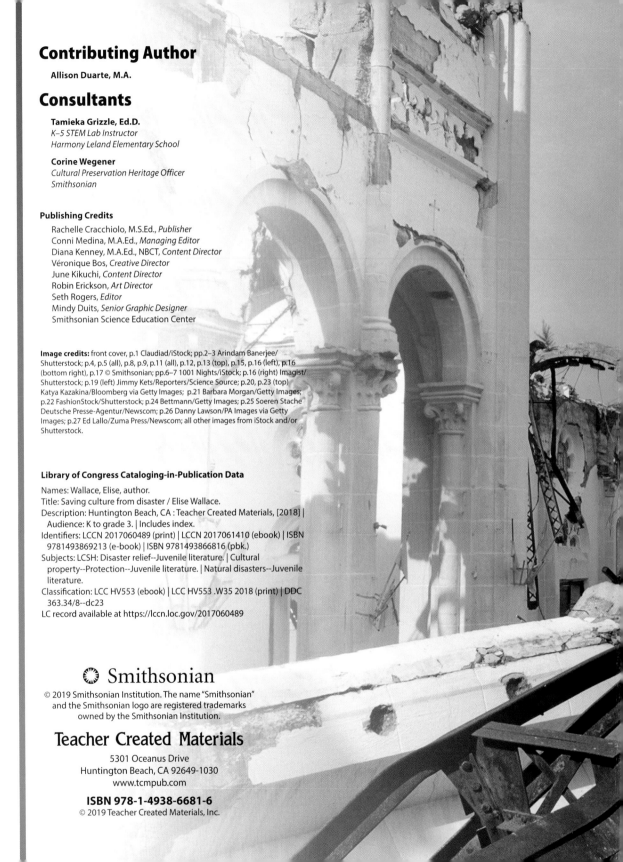

Contributing Author

Allison Duarte, M.A.

Consultants

Tamieka Grizzle, Ed.D.
K–5 STEM Lab Instructor
Harmony Leland Elementary School

Corine Wegener
Cultural Preservation Heritage Officer
Smithsonian

Publishing Credits

Rachelle Cracchiolo, M.S.Ed., *Publisher*
Conni Medina, M.A.Ed., *Managing Editor*
Diana Kenney, M.A.Ed., NBCT, *Content Director*
Véronique Bos, *Creative Director*
June Kikuchi, *Content Director*
Robin Erickson, *Art Director*
Seth Rogers, *Editor*
Mindy Duits, *Senior Graphic Designer*
Smithsonian Science Education Center

Image credits: front cover, p.1 Claudiad/iStock; pp.2–3 Arindam Banerjee/
Shutterstock; p.4, p.5 (all), p.8, p.9, p.11 (all), p.12, p.13 (top), p.15, p.16 (left), p.16
(bottom right), p.17 © Smithsonian; pp.6–7 1001 Nights/iStock; p.16 (right) Imagist/
Shutterstock; p.19 (left) Jimmy Kets/Reporters/Science Source; p.20, p.23 (top)
Katya Kazakina/Bloomberg via Getty Images; p.21 Barbara Morgan/Getty Images;
p.22 FashionStock/Shutterstock; p.24 Bettmann/Getty Images; p.25 Soeren Stache
Deutsche Presse-Agentur/Newscom; p.26 Danny Lawson/PA Images via Getty
Images; p.27 Ed Lallo/Zuma Press/Newscom; all other images from iStock and/or
Shutterstock.

Library of Congress Cataloging-in-Publication Data

Names: Wallace, Elise, author.
Title: Saving culture from disaster / Elise Wallace.
Description: Huntington Beach, CA : Teacher Created Materials, [2018] |
    Audience: K to grade 3. | Includes index.
Identifiers: LCCN 2017060489 (print) | LCCN 2017061410 (ebook) | ISBN
    9781493869213 (e-book) | ISBN 9781493866816 (pbk.)
Subjects: LCSH: Disaster relief--Juvenile literature. | Cultural
    property--Protection--Juvenile literature. | Natural disasters--Juvenile
    literature.
Classification: LCC HV553 (ebook) | LCC HV553 .W35 2018 (print) | DDC
    363.34/8--dc23
LC record available at https://lccn.loc.gov/2017060489

☀ Smithsonian

Teacher Created Materials

5301 Oceanus Drive
Huntington Beach, CA 92649-1030
www.tcmpub.com

ISBN 978-1-4938-6681-6
© 2019 Teacher Created Materials, Inc.

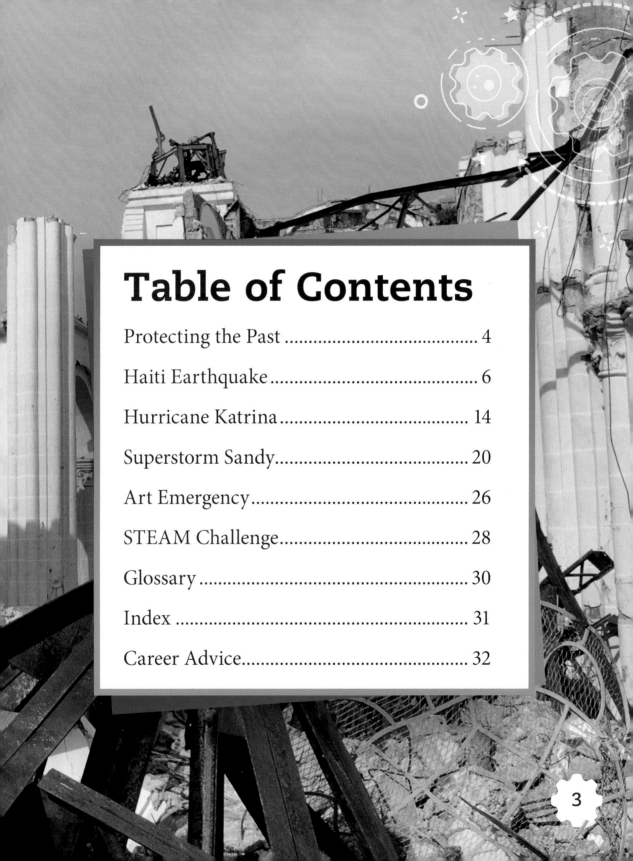

Table of Contents

Protecting the Past

The past is all around us. It can be found in art and in buildings. It can even be found in street signs and in personal items. History is everywhere you look. But what happens when there is a disaster, such as a flood or an earthquake? History can be lost. It can be washed away. That is why it is key to protect the past during times of **crisis**.

People called **conservators** (kuhn-SUHR-vuh-tuhrz) visit places hit by disasters. They look for items that represent the local **culture**. The items might be pieces of art. Or they might be parts of buildings or items from a destroyed museum.

Conservators know the importance of the past. They know that the past tells us where we have been. The past reminds us of our progress. It tells us how our culture has grown and changed.

A conservator carries art pulled from rubble.

A conservator looks at an iron sculpture under a microscope.

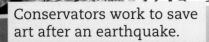

Conservators work to save art after an earthquake.

Haiti Earthquake

Conservators work in tough places. They work in places that have had major disasters. In 2010, Haiti (HAY-tee) faced great loss. A strong earthquake shook the ground. It knocked down many buildings.

Haiti has a big **population**. Most of the people who live there are poor. Many of them do not have jobs. They were not prepared to deal with a disaster.

Over 200,000 people died in the quake. Many were left homeless. But it was not just lives and homes that were lost. Culture was also lost. Museums were destroyed. Libraries and churches were ruined. Each of these places was home to books and artwork. Much of the country's culture was lost. But some things were saved. Conservators worked hard to find and save key pieces of culture.

Almost one-third of the people in Haiti were affected by the earthquake.

Conservators focused their work on a few sites. One of those sites was a church. It was home to 14 murals. These murals were works of art. They had been painted on the walls of the church by famous Haitian (HAY-shuhn) artists.

Only three murals were left after the earthquake. They were badly damaged. Saving them would not be easy. Conservators had to work carefully. They had to choose the best way to save the murals.

First, they had to secure the building. They could not save the artwork if the building fell down! Then, they tested some of the mural fragments. Conservators took these broken pieces to a lab. The tests would show what kind of paint had been used on the murals.

TECHNOLOGY

Building Support

Structural engineers came to the church before any work was done. Their job was to make sure the building was safe. They saw a few problems. There were long cracks in the church walls. The cement that held the walls in place was also crumbling. They decided that scaffolding needed to be built. Scaffolding is made of wooden planks and metal poles. It provides support to buildings so workers can do their jobs without the walls falling down.

9

The tests showed that the murals had been painted with tempera (TEM-puh-ruh) paint. Artists have used this type of paint for a very long time. It was used on murals in ancient tombs.

The tempera used on the murals was **fragile**. If the art was not treated with care, it would crumble. The conservators faced a problem. They had to remove the murals and get them to safety. They had to do so without causing harm.

They could try to chip off the painting from the wall. But this would not work. The art would fall apart. Conservators chose to remove whole walls. This solution allowed each mural to be moved safely.

Early tempera paint was made with egg yolk and colored powder. Today, most tempera paint is made from man-made materials.

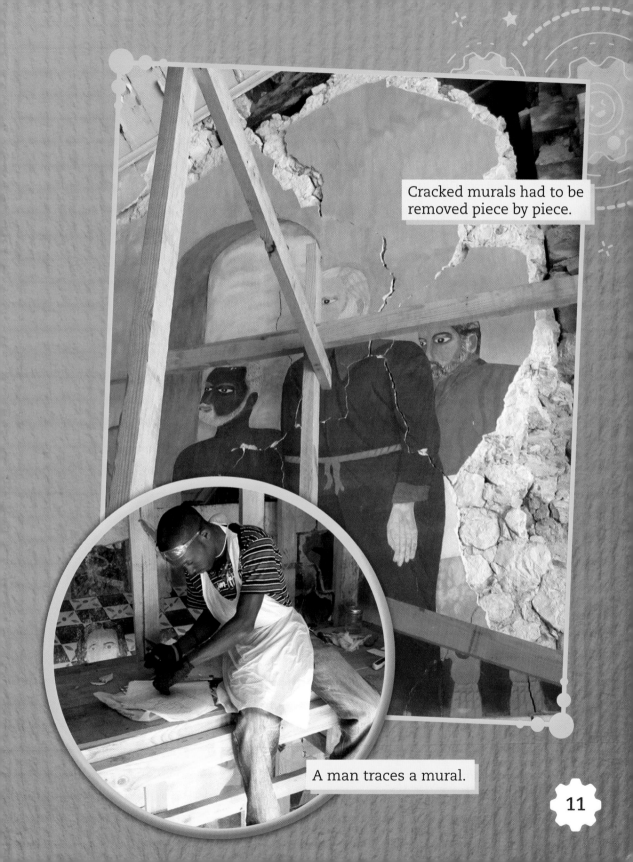

Cracked murals had to be removed piece by piece.

A man traces a mural.

But there were a few more steps before the murals could be removed. The paintings needed to be sprayed with a fixative. This helped the paint bind to stone. That lowered the chance of crumbling.

Workers ran tests to find out which type of fixative would work best. They tried to find a substance that would keep the murals stable. But they did not want to use one that would wreck the art.

In time, a good fixative was found. But there were still more steps to protect the murals. Wooden structures called lattices were built. They were used to hold the art in place as stone was chiseled away. At last, the murals were removed, piece by piece.

Later, the fixative and lattice were removed. This revealed the murals underneath. In the future, the murals will be reassembled. The murals will then be included in the church after it has been rebuilt.

An artist works to match color to one of the murals in need of repair.

Pieces of a mural are laid out to study.

ENGINEERING

Creating a Stable Future

The buildings in Haiti are fragile. Some people say there is not enough money to make stable structures. But there *are* cheap options for improving buildings. Walls can be reinforced, or strengthened, with materials such as straw and sand. Builders use netting to keep the hay bales in place and then surround the bales with layers of plaster.

Hurricane Katrina

In 2005, **Hurricane** Katrina hit the Gulf Coast of the United States. Many people lost their homes. Buildings and towns were ruined.

The hurricane began as a tropical storm. As its wind speed increased, the storm gained power. In just a few days, a hurricane formed.

The city of New Orleans in Louisiana suffered the most. It was covered in water. Streets, cars, and homes were flooded. Many people were stranded. But the danger did not end once the storm passed. People did not have food and water. More than 1,800 people died as a result of the storm.

Hurricane Wind Scale

Category 1 119–153 km/h winds	minimal damage to unanchored mobile homes, vegetation, and signs	
Category 2 154–177 km/h winds	moderate damage to mobile homes, roofs, and small boats; some flooding	
Category 3 178–208 km/h winds	extensive damage to small buildings and low roads; more flooding	
Category 4 209–251 km/h winds	extreme damage to roofs, roads, and boats; homes flooded and mobile homes destroyed	
Category 5 252 + km/h winds	extreme damage to roofs and roads; homes flooded and mobile homes destroyed; tornadoes form	

Source: nhc.noaa.gov/aboutsshws.php

flood watermark

Reading the Water

Floods leave their mark even after they have gone. These are called *watermarks*. Experts can look at the marks and learn more about a flood. They can "read" the watermarks by measuring them. When a watermark is thick, it means that the flood stayed at the same level for a long time. But if a watermark is thin, it means that the flood stayed at that level for a short time.

When experts came to New Orleans, they had a **mission**. They wanted to save damaged items. These items would help tell the story of the storm. The experts were not there to restore items. They wanted to **document** the damage. That may sound odd. Why would a conservator want to keep damaged items? The storm is a key part of New Orleans' past. It is important for people in the future to know what the storm was like.

Many objects that had been damaged by the flood were gathered. Some of the things had to do with music. The city is famous for its strong ties to music. It is known for jazz music. Old records, sheet music, and pictures of famous musicians were collected.

damage caused by Katrina

instruments damaged by Katrina

Some of the damage from Katrina could have been avoided. There are ways to keep buildings safe during floods. Some are quick fixes. Others are big projects that cost a lot of money.

One quick fix is to make roofs that are wind **resistant**. These roofs can hold up in strong winds of a big storm. Another quick fix is to use sandbags. They can keep low-level water out. They stop water from coming into buildings.

Since Katrina, engineers have worked hard to floodproof New Orleans. They have made huge structures called levees (LEH-vees). Levees are designed to block water during floods. This helps the city recover faster. It also lessens the damage.

This levee holds back floodwater.

This floating house has a wind-resistant roof.

This house is made out of shipping containers.

ARTS

Avoiding Damage in Style

There are many ways to prevent flood damage. Some people build houses that keep water away. They put houses on stilts. Others make homes that can float. Some of these floating houses are works of modern art. They have fantastic designs that are appealing to the eye. Others are more simple. They are made from old shipping containers.

Superstorm Sandy

New York City is known for its bright lights. It is called the "city that never sleeps." But many of those lights went out when a huge storm hit in 2012. Millions of people did not have electricity for days. Homes and buildings flooded. Many people died because of the storm.

Superstorm Sandy caused great damage. New York City is known for its art. Many small museums lost art due to flooding.

Other places were affected, too. One of the oldest dance studios in the country was wrecked by the storm. Some of the world's greatest dancers had performed with the Martha Graham Dance Company. The dance studio had a large **archive** (AHR-kyv) of costumes. It also had set pieces from shows. Some were nearly one hundred years old.

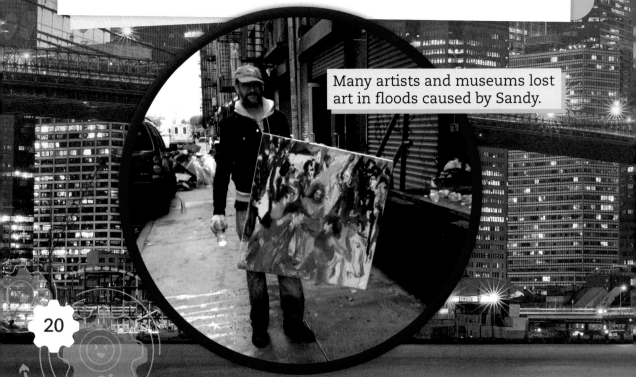

Many artists and museums lost art in floods caused by Sandy.

Martha Graham, who was born in 1894, was a great dancer and teacher of dance.

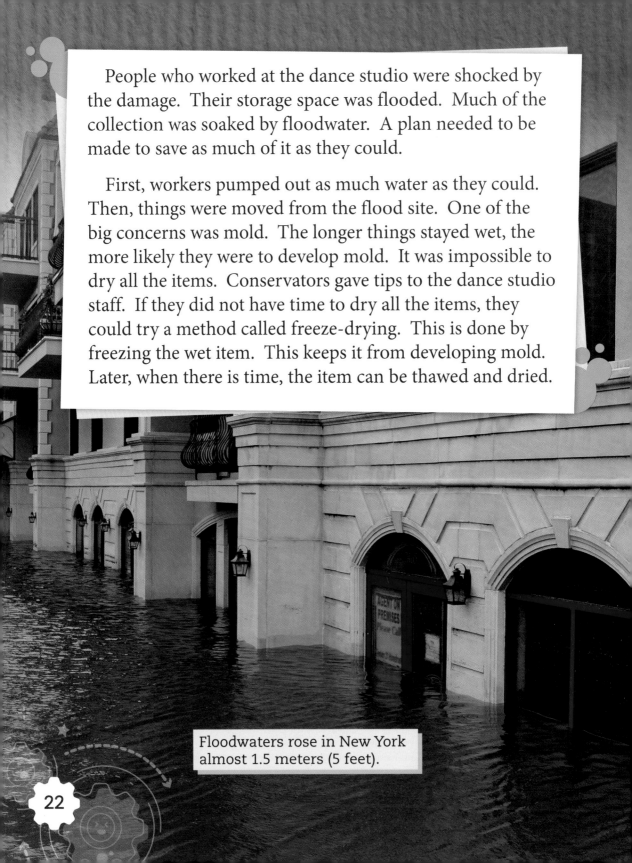

People who worked at the dance studio were shocked by the damage. Their storage space was flooded. Much of the collection was soaked by floodwater. A plan needed to be made to save as much of it as they could.

First, workers pumped out as much water as they could. Then, things were moved from the flood site. One of the big concerns was mold. The longer things stayed wet, the more likely they were to develop mold. It was impossible to dry all the items. Conservators gave tips to the dance studio staff. If they did not have time to dry all the items, they could try a method called freeze-drying. This is done by freezing the wet item. This keeps it from developing mold. Later, when there is time, the item can be thawed and dried.

Floodwaters rose in New York almost 1.5 meters (5 feet).

Mold

Mold is not a plant or an animal. It is a type of fungus. It can grow almost anywhere. But mold grows extra fast in places that are warm, damp, and dark. There are thousands of different kinds of mold. Some molds are helpful. They can be used as medicine. Other molds are harmful. They can cause rashes, breathing problems, and lung infections.

In the end, many items were lost. Thousands of costumes could not be saved. Sets were ruined. The items the studio lost were worth millions of dollars.

But there were some things that the storm could not destroy. Dance routines had been created at the studio. Some of the routines were many years old. They represented the history of the studio and of dance as a whole. The routines could never be damaged by the storm! They were safe in the hearts and minds of the dancers who knew them.

Martha Graham and dance students

The Martha Graham School in New York City is the longest-running dance school in the United States.

Art Emergency

Conservators have important jobs. They save culture! They restore damaged items. Their work helps preserve the past. Much would be lost without them.

Some conservators are rescue workers. Once they are called, these experts hop into action. They report to a scene as soon as they can. Conservators are the first responders when there is an art or culture crisis.

This special job was created out of need. Experts saw how much could be lost in just a few hours after a disaster. They knew that when there was a crisis, there needed to be a team that was ready to help. This team is made up of conservators from around the world. They are superheroes for culture!

A conservator restores a painting.

This woman stores an artifact in a box.

College students can help restore culture. They can build their skills through internships.

STEAM CHALLENGE

Define the Problem

A major storm is headed your way. Flooding is expected. The director of an art museum asks you to protect an old photograph. Your task is to design a way to protect a small photograph from the damage a flood might cause.

 Constraints: You may use four different materials to build something that will protect your photograph.

 Criteria: Your device will keep the photo dry for 30 seconds when put underwater.

Research and Brainstorm

How might a flood damage a photograph? What are some ways that conservators have saved items from water damage? What types of materials do they use?

Design and Build

Sketch your design. What purpose will each part serve? What materials will work best? Build the model. Put a photo in your model to test it out. If you don't have a photo, use a drawing on a piece of paper.

Test and Improve

Place your protected photo into an empty container. Fill the container with water. Once it is full, leave the photo for 30 seconds. Remove and observe the photo. Did it work? How can you improve it? Modify your design, and try again.

Reflect and Share

Could you protect the photo with fewer materials? What materials might work better? How would you change your plan if it was a larger piece of artwork?

Glossary

archive—a place in which public records or historical materials are kept

conservators—people who care for and repair cultural items

crisis—a difficult or dangerous situation

culture—the beliefs, customs, and art of a particular place or society

document—to create a record of something

fixative—a substance used to keep things in position or stick them together

fragile—easily broken or damaged

hurricane—a powerful storm with very strong winds and rain

lattices—frames or structures made of crossed wood or metal strips

mission—a task that is very important

population—a group of individuals of the same species that live in the same place at the same time

reassembled—put back together

resistant—not affected or harmed

structural engineers—people who work with the design and construction of structures, such as bridges, buildings, and dams

Index

CAREER ADVICE
from Smithsonian

Do you want to help preserve culture?
Here are some tips to get you started.

"To protect cultural heritage, you work with people who are experts in different areas. As an archaeologist, I work with conservationists, botanists, and other scientists. Together, we conserve and protect artwork, documents, buildings, and much more." —**Dr. Katharyn Hanson, Archaeologist**

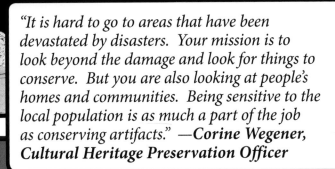

"It is hard to go to areas that have been devastated by disasters. Your mission is to look beyond the damage and look for things to conserve. But you are also looking at people's homes and communities. Being sensitive to the local population is as much a part of the job as conserving artifacts." —**Corine Wegener, Cultural Heritage Preservation Officer**